Success in creating
AI would be the
biggest event in
human history.
Unfortunately, it
might also be the
last, unless we
learn how to avoid
the risks.

STEPHEN HAWKING

Published by
PHD
The Telephone Exchange
5 North Crescent
Chenies Street
London
WC1E 7PH

www.phdmedia.com

First published 2015

Copyright © PHD Worldwide

Author
PHD

Co-authors
Alejandro Clabiorne
Chris Stephenson
Craig Atkinson
Karine Courtemanche
Klint Finley
Malcolm Devoy
Mark Holden
Michael Florence
Phil Rowley
Rohan Tambyrajah
Wayne Bishop
Will Wiseman

Contributors
Alain Desormiers
Anja Hettesheimer
Cedric Lam
Claus Andersen
Dalius Dulevicius
Dirk Fromm
Elda Choucair
Fabian Preiss
Frances Ralston-Good
Haroon Syed
Jason Nebenzahl
Jiří Herian
Joel Pearson
Jyoti Bansal
Kel Hook
Louise Bond
Matias Mateu
Pablo Alonso
Sandra Alvarez
Simon Powlett
Vittorio Bucci

Design
Pen&Pringle

Illustration
Gary Neill

SENTIENCE

THE COMING AI REVOLUTION AND
THE IMPLICATIONS FOR MARKETING

phd

Contents

Introduction: What Exactly is Artificial Intelligence?

If a superior alien civilization sent us a text message saying, 'we'll arrive in a few decades', would we just reply 'okay, call us when you get here, we'll leave the lights on'? Probably not, but that is more or less what has happened with [the way the world is preparing for the advent of] AI.

The potential benefits [of artificial intelligence] are huge; everything that civilization has to offer is a product of human intelligence; we cannot predict what we might achieve when this intelligence is magnified by the tools AI may provide, but the eradication of war, disease, and poverty would be high on anyone's list.

Success in creating AI would be the biggest event in human history.

Unfortunately, it might also be the last, unless we learn how to avoid the risks.

STEPHEN HAWKING [GOOGLE ZEITGEIST. MAY 2015]

The world's religions seek God or gods wherever they may be. The SETI (Search for Extraterrestrial Intelligence) Institute has probed the stars for signs of life beyond our planet. But our first contact with non-human intelligence may happen here on earth, with beings of our own creation.

Artificial intelligence (AI) is here today, and getting smarter every year. With both computing power and data collection increasing exponentially, our machines are gaining on us. Within just over a decade from now they will be far more intelligent than we are.

Computers are already writing stories for major newspapers, helping doctors to search for cures for cancer, and winning game shows. In short, AI has crossed the chasm from science fiction to science fact. Whilst we don't yet have computers as smart as HAL from *2001: A Space Odyssey*, Data from *Star Trek: The Next Generation*, or Samantha from *Her*, futurists like Ray Kurzweil — who's hard at work helping Google build AIs that can understand human language — believe they're just around the corner.

But will these machines actually be sentient? They will certainly appear sentient. Over time we'll develop relationships with them. Business relationships. Personal relationships. Emotional relationships that, even if they're not reciprocated, will feel very real to us.

It's time to start thinking about what this means, both for our lives and, yes, for marketing.

Although AI has largely been the domain of academics and large internet companies, it's starting to trickle down into the consumer sphere, and that's where the most noticeable applications will present themselves. Those applications will be largely ad-supported, meaning that marketing will be one of the first disciplines disrupted by AI.

This may seem like a distant possibility, but the immutable march of Moore's Law — the mega trend in technology that says computers will progressively get twice as fast and cost half as much every 12–18 months — is turning science fiction into a reality in which consumers exist, and in which marketers need to operate.

It's hard to wrap one's head around this type of exponential change, but it illustrates how technology can change so quickly, and why it's so hard to predict the course it will take. Consider this: if a person was to take 30 linear steps along a straight line (1, 2, 3, 4...) they'd end up 30 paces or 30 meters away from their starting point. However, if they took 30 exponential steps (1, 2, 4, 8, 16...) they'd end up one billion meters away or have gone around the planet over 26 times. Now think about that rate of acceleration applied to the speed of computers and you can start to understand Moore's Law. And that's just the beginning. Observers like Ray Kurzweil, the director of engineering at Google, see exponential returns in technological progress as each breakthrough enables even bigger breakthroughs.

That is why we will now start seeing products pop into existence that seem indistinguishable from magic. For example, a universal translator is finally on its way.

Since late 2014, Microsoft has offered a preview version of its popular communication tool Skype that can translate spoken English into Spanish — and vice versa — nearly instantly. It can

WITH BOTH COMPUTING POWER AND DATA COLLECTION INCREASING EXPONENTIALLY, OUR MACHINES ARE GAINING ON US. WITHIN A FEW YEARS THEY MAY BE FAR MORE INTELLIGENT THAN WE ARE also translate text conversations in 40 different languages. It's not perfect, but it works remarkably well. And thanks to the wonders of AI, it will only get better over time.

Skype Translate is one of those things that makes you feel like you're living in the future. And we've been seeing more and more of these types of things every year. We still don't have flying cars, but Google has been developing self-driving cars that have driven over 700,000 miles without any reported incidents. In fact, just about every major automobile company is working on some form of autonomous vehicle — including the driver-on-demand service Uber, who recently revealed that they are building a robotics research lab in Pittsburgh to "kickstart autonomous taxi fleet development."

AI is even starting to impact graphic design. A company called The Grid has automated the process of redesigning websites based on user behavior. Instead of requiring web developers to create multiple versions of a single web design and testing each one to see which performs best, The Grid algorithmically generates website designs based on fundamental design principles and tests the performance of each one. Site owners can decide what behaviors to optimize for, such as e-commerce sales, mailing list sign-ups or video views, and The Grid serves several versions to visitors, recording which ones are best at reaching those goals.

Then there is Google's Now platform, which already anticipates what information we may want or need without us having to search for it. We're informed of airline departure delays, movies we may want to watch and stories we may want to read based on what our social network is consuming and our browser history.

AI is becoming a lot smarter about anticipating human behavior — including purchase decisions. Uber's data team created a model that can predict your exact destination 74 percent of the time before you tell the driver where you're headed. And Amazon has filed a patent for what it calls "Anticipatory Shipping" in which it will begin relocating products to the nearest fulfillment center in anticipation of your order.

Meanwhile, new refrigerators from companies like LG and Samsung can track what groceries you buy, calculate when your produce is about to go bad, and place an order at the supermarket on your behalf. And if you'd rather dine out, new applications like Luka, from a company called 1000 Plateaus, can help find the perfect place by learning your preferences and habits and scanning online reviews and menus.

This new world of intelligent machines will create many new opportunities as well as new challenges for brands. On the one hand, there will be far better tools for finding new audiences and for delivering customized ads to the right customers. But it will also create new challenges, as personal AIs may take the place of traditional advertising for many consumers.

In this book we'll explore the past, present and future of AI and how it will affect not just marketing, but the world as a whole. But before we proceed any further, let's take a step back and ask:

What Exactly is Artificial Intelligence?

John McCarthy, the computer scientist who coined the term in 1956, defined it as "the science and engineering of making intelligent machines."

Most definitions follow along those lines. The problem, however, is defining what we actually mean by "intelligent."

Intelligence has many definitions, but most of them include a few basic ideas: the ability to learn from experience, the ability to apply that learning to new problems, the ability to apply logic and the ability to think abstractly. But what does it mean to think, let alone to think abstractly? What constitutes actual thought — is that something a non-living machine can even do?

Many researchers agree that a machine is intelligent if it can do things that we normally associate with human intelligence. This is a useful definition, but even this can create controversy.

"There's a joke that AI is just whatever a computer can't yet do," says Chris Bishop, a distinguished scientist at Microsoft Research. "There's an element of truth in that. It was once thought that chess would be AI, that it was such a pinnacle of human intellectual achievement that if you could get a machine to play chess everything else would be easy. But then, of course, we built chess-playing computers."

The problem is that most of today's AI systems have narrow applications. Take Google Chauffeur, the AI behind the company's self-driving cars, for example. It slows down when the cars ahead of you hit the brakes, it brakes for pedestrians, and it's a stickler for traffic laws — it's never gotten a ticket. But, unlike a human — or even a dog — it can't learn to do anything other than what it was designed to learn. Chauffeur is great at learning about driving, but it can't learn to play chess, or write news stories, or analyze x-rays.

There are those who argue that an AI isn't truly intelligent unless it can match the human intellect in knowledge and adaptability. The ultimate test of this type of intelligence, for now, is called the "Turing Test." The concept, developed by computer science pioneer Alan Turing, is that rather than asking "can machines think?", we should ask: "can a computer fool a panel of human judges into believing that it's human?" If so, then we might as well consider it to be a thinking machine.

During a Turing Test, the judges would ask the machine, as well as a few humans, a series of questions through a text-only medium, such as email. If the machine can fool the humans into thinking that it's a human, then it's passed the test. Though all purported successes have been controversial, some AIs are getting closer to passing the test. For example, in June 2014, "Eugene Goostman", an AI computer program developed to simulate a 13-year-old boy, managed to convince 33 percent of the judges at the Royal College of London that it was human. This was hailed by some in the press as the first AI to pass the Turing Test, though many experts discounted the result because the judges assumed its strange answers and general lack of knowledge were largely due to "Eugene" being a young boy who didn't speak native English.

Some people prefer the term "machine learning" when talking about software that can learn, but not pass a Turing Test. Others use the term "strong AI" or "general AI" to refer to this sort of human-level or better AI; and "narrow AI" or "weak AI" to refer to those systems that are designed to learn within a single domain, like the self-driving car or Skype Translate.

All AI and machine learning depend on algorithms

— programs that run our Facebook feeds, decide whether we're worthy of loans, and tell us what to watch on Netflix. They sound ominous, but an algorithm is just a step-by-step series of instructions to be completed in order to solve a problem or produce a result. And though many algorithms are indeed very complex, the basic concept is quite simple. You can think of an algorithm as something like a recipe, or substitute the word "process" or "procedure" for the word "algorithm" to understand the concept.

For the purposes of this book, we'll use the term artificial intelligence or AI to refer to both types of AI, and the terms "general AI" and "narrow AI" to refer to each specific type.

Many of today's AI applications are based on simulations of human brain cells called artificial neural networks. These networks don't try to perfectly replicate the form and function of the human brain, but they do draw inspiration from it.

Neural networks, which have been around since the 1950s, are one of the earlier methods for developing AI, but they're not the only approach. As we'll explain later ("The Road to Intelligence", p 21), neural networks faded in popularity among researchers in the 1970s (before making a big come-back in the 1980s), leaving room for other approaches collectively known as symbolic AI. These methods don't seek inspiration from the structure of the brain, and instead focus on statistical modeling. Today, software companies tend to use a mix of both neural networks and symbolic AI in their applications.

Historically, AI has been the domain of academics and a small number of large corporations, but

THERE ARE THOSE WHO ARGUE THAT AN AI ISN'T TRULY INTELLIGENT UNLESS IT CAN MATCH THE HUMAN INTELLECT IN KNOWLEDGE AND ADAPTABILITY we're finally starting to see this stuff become a part of our day-to-day lives. That's largely due to three things, according to *Wired* magazine founding editor Kevin Kelly:

1. | Cheaper, more powerful computer processors. As we've mentioned, Moore's Law states that computers get twice as fast and half as expensive every 12–18 months.

2. | An explosion in the amount of data available. Social networks, photo sharing sites and mobile phones are constantly producing data that can be used to train computers to better recognize patterns.

3. | Better algorithms. The publication of a set of neural networking algorithms called the deep learning algorithms in 2006 accelerated the field. We'll explore deep learning in "The Road to Intelligence", p 20.

Thanks to these trends, AI is now finding its way into more and more consumer facing technologies, and the implications for marketers will grow to the point where an understanding of this area is fundamental for driving good business.

So, let's get right into it.

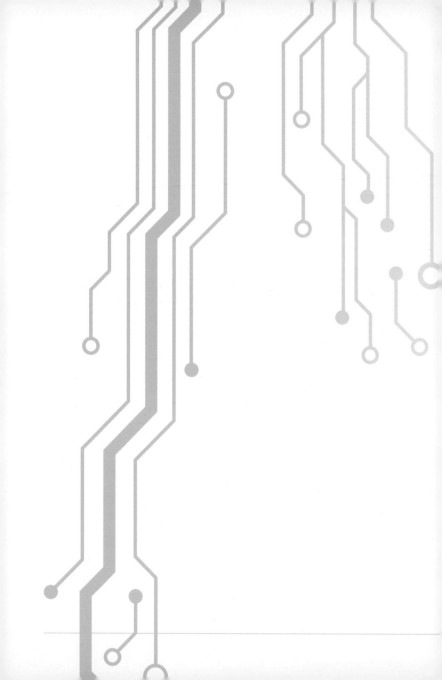

The Road to
Intelligence:
Where It
Started and
the Road
Leading
to Today

The Early Pioneers

AI as we know it today began with a paper
published in 1943 by the eccentric self-taught
mathematician Walter Pitts and University of
Chicago neurophysiologist Warren McCulloch. The
pair were the first to describe the concept of an
artificial neural network and showed that it could
be used to calculate any computable function.
They also suggested that such networks, properly
defined, could learn.

In 1951, Marvin Minsky and Dean Edmonds, then
students at Princeton University, became the first
to build a neural network computer. This primitive
neural network was only able to simulate about 40
neurons, compared to the billions of neurons in the
human brain, but it was a start.

AI, as a specific field of study, was born in
1956, when computer scientist John McCarthy
spearheaded a two-month workshop at Dartmouth
College, along with Minsky and two other students.
The workshop brought together ten researchers

from across the U.S. to study a wide range of topics and show off their work. "The Dartmouth workshop did not lead to any new breakthroughs, but it did introduce all the major figures to each other," Stuart J. Russell and Peter Norvig wrote in their book *Artificial Intelligence: A Modern Approach*. "Perhaps the most lasting thing to come out of the workshop was an agreement to adopt McCarthy's new name for the field: artificial intelligence."

Soon after, a psychologist named Frank Rosenblatt invented a neural networking machine called the Perceptron with backing from the U.S. Navy. He told *United Press International* in 1958 that the machine would be the first non-living thing capable of thought, and he expected the machine to be able to recognize human faces and translate speech or writing from one language to another.

But the expectations were deflated in 1969 by none other than Minsky (who had built the first working neural network less than 20 years before) in a book called *Perceptrons*, co-authored with Seymour Papert.

The book led to a major decrease in funding for neural network research — an event that some people refer to as an "AI winter."

With neural networking all but dead, researchers moved into other directions, attempting to teach machines to learn without modeling their systems on human brains. But in the mid-1980s, a Carnegie Mellon University computer scientist named Geoff Hinton made a major breakthrough in neural networks, overcoming the limitations described in *Perceptrons* by using multiple layers of virtual neurons.

Meanwhile the alternative techniques — generally referred to as "symbolic AI" — proved disappointing, and funding once again flowed in the direction of neural networking. Computers were too slow in the 1980s to take full advantage of Hinton's breakthroughs, but a new generation of neural network researchers soldiered on.

In 2004, Hinton co-founded the Neural Computation and Adaptive Perception Program, aiming to revitalize the field. By 2006, they had created what we now call the deep learning algorithms, and over the next several years the researchers continued to improve their algorithms, and computers grew cheaper and ever more powerful.

Enter, Google

The year 2012 was a banner year for the field. The Google Brain team published a much discussed paper about its neural network that could recognize YouTube videos with cats in them 70 percent of the time. A team of Hinton's students won a competition sponsored by Merck to find molecules that could lead to new pharmaceutical discoveries. And perhaps most impressively, Microsoft showed off its translation system for the first time.

These companies are now in something of a talent war, fiercely competing to hire as many deep learning experts as they possibly can. Google hired Hinton in 2013, then acquired deep learning startup DeepMind for $400,000 in 2014. Facebook hired Hinton's colleague Yann LeCun in 2013 to head the company's newly formed AI research group. And Chinese search giant Baidu poached Google Brain's lead researcher Andrew Ng in 2014.

HUMAN BRAINS ARE STILL FAR TOO COMPLEX TO REPRODUCE WITH COMPUTERS, BUT RESEARCHERS ARE ABLE TO CREATE SIMPLE SIMULATIONS OF THE CONNECTIONS BETWEEN NEURONS CALLED ARTIFICIAL NEURAL NETWORKS

Deep learning has gone from the fringes to the hottest job skill on the market in a few years.

Google announced in early 2014 that it had just completed the mapping of the exact location of every business, every household, and every street number in the entirety of France. You might think Google would have needed to send a large team of people out to each suburb and district with a GPS and that the whole project would have taken a considerable amount of time. However, it took Google one hour.

Google used machine learning algorithms, which means that rather than telling the computer exactly what to look for, you give it some examples and it finds the patterns on its own. In this case, Google took its street-view database — hundreds of millions of images — and had somebody manually go through a few hundred images and circle the street numbers in them. Then Google's engineers wrote a program that said, essentially, "You figure out what's unique about those circled things, find them in the other 100 million images, and then read the numbers that you find."

The massive AI infrastructure the engineers fed those photos into is unofficially called Google Brain, a cluster of thousands of computer servers working in concert to emulate certain aspects of the human brain. And it's not just the Google Maps team that uses Google Brain. According to *Wired*, 30 or 40 different teams at the company are using the system for everything from improving voice recognition on mobile phones to automatically sorting images as part of Google Image Search.

DEEP LEARNING HAS GONE FROM THE FRINGES TO THE HOTTEST JOB SKILL ON THE MARKET IN A FEW YEARS

What Exactly Is Deep Learning?

No one knows quite how the human brain works, but we do know that it's made up of billions of cells called neurons, and that the complex connections between these cells give rise to human intelligence, including our ability to learn, remember, and solve problems.

Human brains are still far too complex to reproduce with computers, but researchers are able to create simple simulations of the connections between neurons called "artificial neural networks." These neural networking computers don't come anywhere near human consciousness, but they can spot patterns and solve problems.

Deep learning refers both to a set of algorithms for creating neural networks, and to the field of study within artificial intelligence dedicated to creating, studying and using those algorithms.

Perhaps the most important thing that the deep learning algorithms make possible is the creation of neural networks that learn with little to no feedback from humans. For example, if you wanted to teach a traditional neural network to tell the difference between dogs and cats, you would feed many photos of dogs and cats into the computer and label each one with either the term "dog" or the term "cat." Eventually, with enough examples, it should be able to recognize a photo of a dog or cat and label it on its own.

But with deep learning, you would simply give the computer as many photos of dogs and cats as you can, and it will eventually figure out how to classify photos into the two categories on its own. As psychologist Gary Marcus wrote in The New Yorker, it's a bit like giving a child a pile of blocks, and asking her to sort them into categories without giving her any instructions, relying on her own ability to recognize similarities and create her own categories.

But your examples have to be representative of what you want the machines to learn. "When teaching computers to recognize dogs, for example, I need to make sure not all of the photos have grass in them, so that it doesn't learn the wrong lesson," Pete Warden, the founder of a deep learning company called Jetpac that was acquired by Google, told *Wired* in 2014. "It's a bit like being a computer teacher, with a lesson plan and all."

Deep learning is most effective when there are huge numbers of examples that can be used to train the neural network. That's why the techniques have become so popular with large web companies like Google and Facebook, which have massive troves of data on which to train the algorithms.

Although deep learning is new, neural networking actually dates back to the very beginning of AI. But for many years, it remained on the outskirts of AI research. Now, thanks to deep learning, neural networking is back at the forefront of the field.

The secret behind Google Brain is a new AI discipline called "deep learning," — the same set of techniques that power Microsoft's Skype Translate and Facebook's eerily accurate facial recognition system that tags your friends in your photos without you having to tell it who's actually in the picture. More than any other technology, deep learning is enabling the development of useful AI.

Going Deeper

Deep learning has advanced the state of the art in AI considerably. But it's a long way from creating machines that think like humans. That's because although deep learning algorithms are inspired in part by the human brain, they actually function quite differently.

"What we really need," says Jeff Hawkins, founder of the AI company Numenta, "is a new type of neural networking that more closely reproduces the actual structure of the human brain." And he says his company is well on its way to creating just that.

Hawkins is better known for creating the hand-held computer company Palm in 1992. But since 2002, he's been on a quest to unlock the secrets of the brain. "If we can figure out how brains work," he says, "then we can figure out how to build intelligent machines."

Hawkins and the team at Numenta have created an approach to AI that they call "hierarchical cortical memory." They're trying to simulate a part of the brain called the neocortex, which handles sensory perception, thought, language, spatial reasoning, and much more. The papers they've published have been well received in the AI community. Dag Kittlaus, one of the founders of Apple's Siri and co-founder of the AI company Viv "Conversational Computing" p 37 says he's a big fan of Hawkins and his approach. "They've done a ton of research," Kittlaus says. "But the proof will be in killer apps."

It remains to be seen how effective the approach will be in the real world. Numenta has created a piece of software called Grok, a tool that helps information technology departments maintain computer servers, but Hawkins says that this product is only scraping the surface of what will eventually be possible. "No one can tell you what the applications are going to be, no one at any point can tell you what the applications are going to be 20 years from now," he says.

Google, meanwhile, is banking on combining deep learning with a new approach called "reinforcement learning," a concept pioneered by Demis Hassabis, Shane Legg and Mustafa Suleyman, the co-founders of DeepMind.

Reinforcement learning helps machines learn in much the same way we do: by repeating the same tasks again and again until we get them right. Hassabis spent years working on practical AI systems for video games such as *Black and White* and *Theme Park* before returning to university to study neuroscience. It was this academic work that led him to the conclusion that AI research had been too narrow in its emulation of the brain.

"Deep learning is about essentially [mimicking the] cortex," he told Backchannel in 2015. "But the hippocampus is another critical part of the brain and it's built very differently, a much older structure. If you knock it out, you don't have memories."

By adding deep reinforcement to deep learning — an approach Hassabis calls "deep reinforcement learning" — Google hopes to overcome many of the limitations of deep learning. And it's working.

In February 2015, Hassabis and his team at Google created an algorithm that can learn to play old Atari 2600 video games, and play them as well as humans. Instead of having to create a new algorithm for each game — as most AI researchers have done in the past — the researchers simply tell their game-playing algorithms to optimize their behavior for the highest score. After 500 attempts at playing the games, the algorithms are super-human players. It may still be technically "weak AI", but it's most certainly a big step towards creating a more general strong AI.

Ultimately, a multi-pronged approach to AI may be necessary — one that combines deep learning, cortical memory alongside the more traditional symbolic AI.

Intelligence on Demand

Ken Jennings won 74 episodes in a row of the game show *Jeopardy* in 2004. He still holds the record for the longest winning streak in the show's history, making him one of the greatest *Jeopardy* champions of all time.

But even before Jennings had finished his original winning streak, a team of researchers at IBM were plotting a way to beat him. They would train a challenger with far more facts committed to memory than even Jennings ever could.

That challenger was, of course, IBM's Watson, probably the best known artificially intelligent computer in the world. It would go on to beat both Jennings and his fellow *Jeopardy* champion Brad Rutter over the course of three episodes in February 2011, and show the world just how far the idea of AI had already come.

Today, IBM wants Watson to do far more than play games. IBM has invested $1 billion into a business unit dedicated to commercializing the technology. Watson is already helping researchers at the Memorial Sloan Kettering Cancer Center in New York City search for cancer treatments, as well as working with ANZ bank in Australia to analyze customer financial data to make smarter recommendations for wealth management. But its real future might be in providing behind-the-scenes intelligence for a whole new generation of applications that we're only just beginning to imagine.

Watson wasn't the first IBM supercomputer to beat human champions in a game that most people thought machines couldn't win. In 1997, IBM's DeepBlue beat chess grand master Garry Kasparov in an equally well-publicized event. Like Watson, DeepBlue was part of a long tradition at IBM called "Grand Challenges," aimed to push IBM researchers to accomplish new feats of engineering, and educate the public about the possibilities of technology.

Unlike Watson, DeepBlue was never repurposed for the business world. In fact, most of IBM's Grand Challenge projects have never been commercialized. What's unique about Watson among other IBM projects is that it's so universally useful. Yes, the rules of *Jeopardy* are weird. But, ironically, preparing Watson to play such an idiosyncratic show may be what made Watson so applicable to other scenarios.

Jeopardy questions come in the form of answers, with contestants expected to respond in the form of a question. For example: "William Wilkinson's 'An account of the principalities of Wallachia and Moldavia' inspired this author's most famous novel."

Watson correctly responded: "Who is Bram Stoker?"

To pull this off, Watson searches a vast database of indexed text and prepares a list of possible answers. It then judges the likelihood of each possible answer being correct, and then states the one it deems most likely to be correct.

It's similar in many ways to a search engine, which also crawls text and ranks possible responses in a particular order. Instead of pointing you to a set of web pages that might contain the answer to your question, Watson has to construct a grammatically correct answer.

The important part of teaching Watson how to parse *Jeopardy* questions was teaching it how to learn from its mistakes, so the researchers didn't have to prepare the machine for every possible way a question — or in this case, answer — could be phrased. And because Watson can learn, it can be taught to do things besides answer trivia questions.

It would be a mistake to think that Watson "understands" these questions the way that humans do. In fact, IBM prefers the term "cognitive computing" to AI, to avoid confusion with human-level general AIs. But for a narrow AI, Watson can adapt to some pretty broad scenarios.
For example, IBM has partnered with Twitter to help markets make sense of the ocean of data the social networking company collects. "It can provide insight into what trends are, so they can better understand

the market," John Gordon, the vice president of IBM's Watson group says. "Watson will help people target the right areas, or change products so that they're more attractive."

But a potentially more transformative idea is a cloud-based version of Watson that will allow computer programmers to develop and build new applications that can ask Watson questions behind-the-scenes.

One of the first new applications for Watson comes courtesy of healthcare company Pathway Genomics. Pathway offers a smart phone app that enables users to pull health data from a variety of sources — such as personal health records and wearable fitness trackers like the Fitbit — into one place. Watson then takes that data, and produces customized diet and exercise recommendations, such as what they should eat for dinner based on how many calories they've already eaten that day.

But this is just one of many different possibilities for the cloud service, and many more will soon arise. And IBM's not the only company to realize the potential value of providing AI — or cognitive computing, if you will — as a service to other programmers. Microsoft is already offering its AzureML service, while startup CognitiveScale has its own Watson-based service that aims to expand Watson's capabilities.

Soon anyone will be able to tap into these vast AI resources on demand.

Ray Kurzweil: The Singularitarian

While the first AI summit was happening at Dartmouth in the summer of 1956, an eight-year-old inventor named Ray Kurzweil was busy building a robotic puppet show.

A few years later, at the age of 12, he built his first computer. By 1965 Kurzweil, whose father was a musician, was on national television showing off a computer that could generate original musical compositions. In high school he corresponded with AI pioneer Marvin Minsky, and later studied under him at Massachusetts Institute of Technology (MIT), where Kurzweil received a bachelor's degree in computer science and literature.

Unsurprisingly, Kurzweil grew up to become one of the most important voices in the AI industry. As a director of engineering at Google he's guiding the company's efforts to teach computers to understand natural language. But he's most famous for his theory that humanity is fast approaching the point at which not only are our machines more intelligent than we are, but we merge our own consciousness with them, after which point it's impossible to predict how technology — and humanity — will develop. He calls this the "Singularity," and he believes we will reach this point by 2045 at the latest.

That may sound far-fetched, but Kurzweil is no mere dreamer. He has done plenty of practical work in the technology industry, and earned a National Medal of Technology from President Bill Clinton in 1999.

Perhaps his most important invention was the Kurzweil Reading Machine (KRM), first released in 1976, a tool that can scan text and read it out loud — a major boon to the blind. In order to build the KRM, however, he had to create several other things first: software that could recognize text typed in many different fonts, the first flatbed scanner, and the first text-to-speech synthesizer to actually read the text back to the user.

Stevie Wonder, one of the first people to buy the KRM, inspired his next project: creating audio synthesizers that sound like real instruments. This resulted in the creation of the Kurzweil 250 synthesizer.

Two themes are apparent in Kurzweil's inventions. First, these inventions give machines new capabilities, such as the ability to see, hear, speak, and make music. Second, and more importantly, each of these inventions also extends the user's capabilities, enabling humans to do things we couldn't previously do.

Kurzweil also has an impressive track record for predictions. In his 1990 book *The Age of Intelligent Machines*, Kurzweil predicted that a computer would beat a human chess champion by 1998. IBM's supercomputer DeepBlue beat world champion chess master Garry Kasparov in 1997. He also predicted the rise of the internet, search engines, and the availability of ubiquitous wireless networks. That might not seem like much of a prediction, but keep in mind that in 1990 the internet wasn't yet available to the general public, and mobile phones were still hefty bricks used by only elite business people.

But it's the predictions in Kurzweil's next book, *The Age of Spiritual Machines* that he's best known for today.

The term "singularity" is borrowed from physics, where it describes the center of a black hole, where gravity is theoretically infinite and all ability to make any predictions breaks down. Mathematician and science fiction author Vernor Vinge first used the term to apply to technology in 1993, referring to the way that advances in fields like AI and biology could alter humanity to such a degree that we can no longer recognize ourselves and change will occur at such a fast rate that all predictions will break down.

While researching *Spiritual Machines*, Kurzweil became convinced that we're on the brink of the singularity. He argues that technology progresses exponentially, and that based on current rates of change, we should see human-level intelligent machines by 2029, and the singularity by 2045.

Of course, not everyone agrees with Kurzweil's predictions. Biologists such as PZ Meyers and David J. Linden have criticized the inventor's understanding of the brain and human biology. "I contend that our understanding of biological processes remains on a stubbornly linear trajectory," Linden wrote on the blog *Boing Boing*. "In my view the central problem here is that Kurzweil is conflating biological data collection with biological insight."

Kurzweil's track record as a prognosticator has also been called into question. Journalist Daniel Lyons, writing for Newsweek, points out that not all of Kurzweil's predictions have been so great. In *Spiritual Machines* — published at the height of the dotcom boom — Kurzweil predicted that the economy would keep soaring through 2029. Instead, we saw major stock market busts in both 2000 and 2008. He also predicted that a publicly traded company would reach a market capitalization of $1 trillion by 2009. As of this writing (January, 2015), Apple holds the record for highest market capitalization ever, having reached $700 billion in November 2014.

Kurzweil also predicted that by 2009 computers would become increasingly invisible, having been embedded into our clothes, watches or eye glasses and that spoken word interfaces would replace keyboards for most textual input. We may be headed in that direction thanks to wearable computers and new technologies such as Microsoft's HoloLens, but we're certainly not where Kurzweil predicted we'd be by 2009.

Part of what makes Kurzweil's predictions so hard to swallow is the parade of predecessors who have made grandiose claims about AI before him. For example, Stuart J. Russell and Peter Norvig quote political scientist and early AI researcher Herbert Simon, speaking in 1957: "It is not my aim to surprise or shock you — but the simplest way I can summarize is to say that there are now in the world machines that think, that learn and that create. Moreover, their ability to do these things is going to increase rapidly until — in a visible future — the range of problems they can handle will be coextensive with the range to which human mind has been applied."

But Kurzweil is more data driven than his predecessors, and despite a few duds, he's been remarkably prescient if not in how quickly technology would be adopted, then at least how quickly it's been developed. And that's no small thing, especially with 2029 looming close.

Conversational Computing

While Kurzweil dreams of merging our consciousness with machines, and new Watson-powered applications trickle out to the market, millions of smart phone users are already using artificially intelligent virtual assistants every day.

And though Apple's Siri, Google Now, and Microsoft's Cortana are state of the art in digital virtual assistants today, Siri's creators are working on an even more advanced AI system that they hope will be able not just to do what you ask, but to understand what you're asking as well.

Siri began its artificial life at the research institute SRI International as part of a project called "Cognitive Assistant that Learns and Organizes," (CALO).

The CALO project was one of the best funded AI research projects in history, with a total of $150 million from Defense Advanced Research Projects Agency (DARPA) — the same U.S. Defense Department agency that funded the creation of the internet. The project engaged 300 researchers and spanned 25 research institutions, with SRI acting as the central point of contact. The ultimate goal of CALO was to create machines that could help military officers organize and prioritize information, allocate resources, juggle appointments and much more.

The project's leader, Adam Cheyer, was by all accounts a genius, and his work at CALO was ground-breaking. But he didn't quite know what to do with it. Fortunately, another SRI employee, Dag Kittlaus, did.

Kittlaus came to SRI from Motorola, where he ran the company's smart phone division. At Motorola, Kittlaus worked with Android — back before it was acquired by Google — on what was to be the first smart phone powered by the company's operating system. He left Motorola after the company dropped the project, but he had seen the future, and it was mobile.

"At the time Google and search was all the rage," he says. "I could have made it a smarter search engine, but we wanted to look further ahead."

Instead of a better search engine, Kittlaus and company came up with the idea of using CALO as the foundation of a virtual personal assistant for smart phones.

Voice-activated controls for everything from lights to home stereo systems had already existed for decades, enabling users to do things like turn appliances on or off or even change the channel on the television. But Cheyer's team had developed a system that could do much more. "Voice recognition is not the same as AI," Kittlaus explains. "Voice recognition is turning sounds into words. That's what people were doing back then, but what we were working on is understanding what those words meant, finding the context, and then building a platform that connected it to the web."

That is to say, Siri doesn't just translate a voice command into a digital signal and turn the lights on or off. It's able to parse sentences and phrases to determine what actions you want it to perform.

Siri was spun-out of SRI as an independent company in 2007 and released its first iPhone app in 2010. Apple bought Siri the next year and integrated it deeply into the iPhone's operating system. But along the way, Apple also scaled back Siri's abilities.

Although the Apple version of Siri can handle basic tasks like adding appointments to your calendar and setting your alarm, it has mostly become exactly what Kittlaus didn't want it to be: a search engine. The team originally envisioned a tool that would allow users to control all sorts of apps through just a single interface simply by telling Siri what they wanted done.

"That was the original vision," laments Kittlaus. "But Apple hasn't chosen to pursue it, at least not since Steve Jobs died."

Meanwhile, Apple's competitors weren't sitting still. By November 2010 Microsoft already had a capable voice recognition function in its Xbox 360 video game console thanks to the Kinect product, and more recently the company has made the leap into mobile virtual assistants with Cortana, competing with Apple head-on.

OUR KIDS WON'T BE ABLE TO IMAGINE NOT HAVING A DIGITAL PERSONAL ASSISTANT HANDLING THE MUNDANE PARTS OF LIFE, KITTLAUS SAYS

Google released its answer to Siri, Google Now, in July 2012. Now one-upped Siri by not just responding to your voice requests, but proactively anticipating information you might want, much like a human assistant might be able to anticipate your needs. For example, it will nudge you about TV shows it thinks you might want to watch tonight, or let you know what the traffic is like between your office and your home.

Apple may try to catch-up with Google by integrating technology from a company it acquired in 2013 called Cue. Formerly known as Greplin, Cue scanned users' inboxes to help create a customized agenda. Much like Google Now, it attempted to provide information to users before they realized that they needed or wanted it.

But Kittlaus and company want to go even further than Google Now, so they've left Apple and started a brand new company called Viv to pick-up where they left off with Siri.

Kittlaus is still remaining tight-lipped about exactly what the new company is doing, but he did explain that instead of just one app, they plan to let other companies tap into Viv, much as IBM is letting other companies develop and build new apps atop Watson. For example, a travel company could license Viv's technology to make a smart travel agent. "You could tell it: 'find me a good deal to go to the Caribbean with the kids' and it will know who your kids are, what they like to do," Kittlaus says. "It will know the kinds of hotels you like to stay in, what your budget is."

In short, Viv will help companies create a new generation of apps that are able to understand what a user is actually looking for, and why they're looking for it. Meanwhile, Apple, Google and Microsoft are continuing to invest in AI, and each has proven that it's not afraid to spend money on acquisitions. And smaller startups like Kimera Systems are trying to teach virtual assistants to understand our queries. The race to create the first truly intelligent virtual assistant is far from over. But one thing just about everyone agrees on, is that these virtual assistants are here to stay, and they'll only get smarter.

"Our kids won't be able to imagine not having a digital personal assistant handling the mundane parts of life," Kittlaus says.

Robo-bards

Los Angeles residents were roused from sleep by an earthquake the morning of March 17, 2014. Three minutes later, those who reached for their phones, or staggered to their computers, would find a story on the *Los Angeles Times* website telling them exactly what had happened.

"A shallow magnitude 4.7 earthquake was reported Monday morning five miles from Westwood, California, according to the U.S. Geological Survey," it read. "The temblor occurred at 6:25 a.m. Pacific time at a depth of 5.0 miles."

The paper's superhuman response to the quake was enabled by a computer program called Quakebot written by journalist Ken Schwencke, *Slate* reported in 2014. The program watched for alerts from the U.S. Geological Survey — which monitors seismic activity around the world — and automatically generates Mad Libs-style stories from the organization's data. When Schwencke awoke that day, all he had to do was read the story, already written for him, and hit publish.

Welcome to the future of writing.

Quakebot is incredibly simple, as far as software goes. But there are companies with much bigger ambitions, such as Narrative Science, a Chicago-based technology startup.

Narrative Science built a software platform called Quill that acts as a souped-up version of Quakebot. It can monitor data from a variety of different sources and, using AI algorithms developed by the company, turn them into concise news stories that could pass for being human-written.

Quill stories on corporate earnings reports have appeared in publications like *Fortune*, and its sports reporting has graced the digital pages of sites like *Big Ten*. Much like the *LA Times'* earthquake coverage, all of these stories have been computer-generated — and that's just the beginning. The company's co-founder and chief scientist Kris Hammond told *Wired* in 2012 that a computer-generated story would win the Pulitzer Prize within five years.

But Hammond says that Narrative Science's mission isn't to put journalists out of work. In fact, the company actually started out as part of a Northwestern University program that paired computer science students with journalists. Rather, the company wants to use computers to write stories that humans would never have written in the first place. Besides, Narrative Science thinks the real money will come not from newspapers looking to layoff relatively inexpensive reporters, but from companies with huge numbers of spreadsheets and other data that needs to be analyzed, such as financial services companies. And that's much more challenging than just putting together a news story based on sports scores or quarterly earnings.

"Figuring out what's interesting to the user and how to structure it is even more important than the language," Hammond says. "What we're slamming ourselves up against is that people can't look at a spreadsheet and see the world, they can't look at a visualization and understand what's happening."

To demonstrate its value, the company offers a free service that hooks into Google Analytics and produces automated reports that explain, in plain English, what's been going on with your website's traffic.

Narrative Science isn't alone in this endeavor. Other companies, such as Automated Insights and Yseop are also trying to turn the world's structured data into easy-to-read stories.

Perhaps the most interesting possibility for these products is the way they can complement, rather than replace, traditional approaches to research and writing.

A reporter could use Quill to plow through social media data to find inspiration for a story. Future technologies from these companies could make it easier to find the most important nuggets of information in massive document dumps such as Chelsea Manning's leak of classified military and diplomatic documents to Wikileaks, or the Snowden files. It would be up to the human journalists to add context and weave the information into a compelling narrative, but the software could do some of the heavy lifting, separating out the banal from the newsworthy.

Corporate executives, meanwhile, could use these tools for preliminary analysis, before threading those insights into more polished reports that take the company's goals and strategies into account, along with the sort of insight that only humans can bring to the table.

In other words, journalists, market analysts and other people who write for a living probably aren't going to be obsolete any time soon. But there's a growing number of new tools that could transform how they do their jobs.

And non-fiction is just the beginning. A program backed by the European Commission called "The What-If Machine" is designed to brainstorm ideas for fiction, such as "what if there was a little fish who forgot how to swim?" or "what if there was an old person who couldn't find a car that was expensive? But instead, she found a special style of house that was so costly that the

old person didn't want the expensive car anymore."
These aren't exactly Booker Prize material, but
as AI technology progresses tools like this will
only get better. And while computer-generated
literature is still a dream, as we saw in "Ray
Kurzweil: The Singularitarian,"(p 33) composers
have been using computers to generate scores
for decades. Visual artists have also taken to
using tools such as the Processing programming
language to generate graphics and animation.
The next Mozart, Shakespeare or Picasso might
actually be a computer program.

Machine Visionaries

IBM's Watson can digest massive collections of
text and use it to spit out answers on just about
any subject you can imagine. Narrative Science
can write reports on numerous topics with
minimal human input. Siri can scour the web and
tell you what movies are playing at your favorite
theater, or how many brunch restaurants are open
in your neighborhood.

All of these tasks depend on understanding words.
But today's web is increasingly made up of images.

Pinterest, which is almost purely image focused,
remains one of the most popular social media
sites on the web. Facebook's photo sharing app
Instagram surpassed Twitter in total monthly
active users in December 2014. And on Tumblr —
the most popular social network with teenagers
— 75 percent of all posts are images, and 90
percent of those posts have no identifying text
or tags, according to research conducted by
Philadelphia-based analytics company Curalate.

"We think what is happening at a really

fundamental level is that consumers are increasingly electing to communicate in pictures," says Curalate co-founder and CTO Nick Shiftan.

That creates huge new challenges — and opportunities — for brands, and a growing crop of startups are trying to find ways to mine the world of images for new insights that can help brands.

In the beginning of the internet, there was the word. It was available only to a few researchers and educators, who used monochrome, plain-text terminals to play games, swap emails, and pontificate on early forums. Then came the first wave of web browsers, most of which didn't support images at all. The early days of social media were, likewise, heavily text based. LiveJournal, Facebook and Twitter were all about sharing chunks of text with your friends.

That started to change when Pinterest took off in 2011, according to Shiftan.

That was perfect timing for Shiftan and Curalate co-founder and CEO Apu Gupta. Their previous startup idea — a marketplace for storage space that Gupta now describes as "Airbnb for hoarders" — hadn't worked out, and they were looking for a new idea in early 2012. By this point there were already dozens of analytics companies dedicated to helping brands engage consumers on social media, and mine these new services for actionable insights. But while most of them focused on Facebook and Twitter, Shiftan and Gupta saw an opportunity to create a Pinterest analytics service before anyone else.

The problem was that most of the tools on which analytics companies had traditionally relied didn't really apply to an image-based social network.

Take the most basic thing you'd want to do with an image-web analytics engine: find out where pictures from your brand's website are being shared. It's harder than you might think. Comparing two image files to determine if they're the same isn't actually that tough, Shiftan says, but it's extremely difficult to compare one image with millions of other images. Add in the fact that images are often compressed and resized when shared on social media, and you've got a radically complex problem.

Curalate can now determine things such as which of a company's photos are the most popular on the web, enabling companies to highlight the best performing photos on their websites. But there are less obvious uses as well.

"The web was not set up to make sense of images," Shiftan says. "So we want to decode all of that to make better decisions, to better understand consumers and form better relationships."

For example, one of Curalate's customers — a major retailer — had a black dress that was very popular on social media. Curalate discovered that the term "Vegas dress" kept popping up in tags and descriptions of the dress on sites like Pinterest, even though it wasn't the term the retailer used in its own descriptions of the product. Based on Curalate's discovery, the retailer's web team realized they should optimize their site for that search term, and buy search engine advertising for the keyword "Vegas dress."

But one thing Curalate can't yet do is recognize what's in a photo. That's where GazeMetrix comes in. The company is focused on helping brands discover where their logo is popping up online. The company can scan Instagram and find examples of people posting photos of, say, someone drinking your company's brand of beer, or wearing a particular type of sneaker. You can then contact those people and ask for permission to republish their candid photos on your own social media channels, or reward them with gift certificates.

Meanwhile, another company called Clarifai has gone beyond recognizing static images into the realm of video. The company has created technology that can not only watch a video and tell whether it contains a cat or a dog, but it can also identify certain features within a video — such as eyes — and even subjective qualities like cuteness. Facebook is pioneering similar video watching algorithms – and is now able to identify with high levels of confidence (80%+) which sport is being played.

Of course, scanning social media for brand images isn't the only use for advanced machine vision. Companies like Google and Facebook are already investing enormous resources into image recognition software ("Machine Visionaries", p 45). Just last August, Google acquired Jetpac, a startup founded by ex-Apple engineer Pete Warden that attempted to create travel guides by analyzing photos posted to Instagram. Jetpac could, for instance, recognize dog-friendly bars based on the number of dogs that appear in photos taken at the place, or restaurants with outdoor seating based on the presence of lots of blue sky in snap shots. Google discontinued Jetpac's apps after the acquisition, and the team is now presumably hard at work on other projects within Google. But Jetpac's ideas suggest that we're only beginning to scratch the surface of what's possible with image recognition on the web.

And as these systems get better, machine vision will play a huge role in the future, from automatically processing surveillance footage, to helping brands figure out how people engage in their category.

Brain on a Chip

Thus far we've talked mostly about using computer software to simulate certain parts of the human brain. But what about hardware that mimics the brain's structure? Well, that's in the works too.

Companies as varied as IBM, semiconductor company Qualcomm, and aerospace research outfit HRL Laboratories are all working on computer chips based on "neuromorphic" principles — in other words, chips inspired by the structure and function of the brain.

Qualcomm has already used its new chip architecture to teach robots to navigate a grid by giving them positive reinforcement when they land on the correct squares, instead of programming them to follow a particular path. HRL, meanwhile, has invented an aerial drone that can recognize whether it's been in a particular room before.

These tiny chips aren't meant to replace, say, a full-scale IBM Watson system with thousands of processor cores within it. But they might be able to push chip design forward.

Chip makers are under pressure to build faster chips that use less electricity, explains Qualcomm director of product management Samir Kumar. Although chips have gotten exponentially more powerful over the four decades since the first microprocessor was introduced in 1971, faster chips generally guzzle more energy as well. In recent years, the demand for ever-more powerful smart phones and tablets has encouraged the development of more energy efficient chips, but these are seldom as powerful as their more electricity-hungry counterparts. To make real progress in the chip field, these companies would need to find a way to balance power and efficiency. Fortunately, nature has already provided us with an example. "We looked at the brain as something that has enormous computational power but used relatively little energy," Kumar says.

Although computers can do math far faster than we can, there are certain things we still do far better and faster than computers. For example, we can recognize photos of friends almost instantly, even if they're badly distorted or incomplete. That's because the brain contains millions of neurons acting in concert. Of course, computers also have multiple processors working in parallel, but while the largest supercomputer, as of November 2014, has about one million cores, the human brain has billions of neurons and trillions of connections, called synapses, between those neurons.

Individually, these neurons aren't very smart — certainly less powerful than a computer processor. But when they work together, they can outperform even the biggest supercomputers on the market. Computers must be programmed to break complex problems into smaller ones that each processor can tackle on its own. But the human brain is essentially pre-wired to do this. When you look at a photo, for example, you don't need a program telling your brain to route the sensory data coming in from your eyes to the occipital lobe for processing. It all happens automatically and, Kumar explains, this is a big part of why humans are so much better at recognizing images and sounds, or feeling textures, than even the most sophisticated computers available today.

Neuromorphic chips, however, borrow from the brain's design to sense the world around them. For example, as Tom Simonite explained in the MIT Technology Review, the HRL drone chip will produce a unique pattern of connection between the artificial neurons, based on the sensory data it received upon entering a room. When the drone enters the same room again, the same pattern will light up, signaling that this is a room it's been in before. It's a simple trick, but the first step towards building chips that can solve problems without being programmed.

Of course, these chips are nowhere near as complex as the human brain. IBM's TrueNorth chips, for instance, simulate only about one million neurons and 256 million synapses. And though these new designs are inspired by the structures of the human brain, they don't strictly simulate the brain. Much like the deep learning researchers, neuromorphic chip designers are looking to the brain for inspiration, not for a blueprint. Still, these chips are a significant break from traditional microprocessors, and could enable a whole host of new applications.

MUCH LIKE THE DEEP LEARNING RESEARCHERS, NEUROMORPHIC CHIP DESIGNERS ARE LOOKING TO THE BRAIN FOR INSPIRATION, NOT FOR A BLUEPRINT

Qualcomm and IBM are both working with partners on potential applications for these new chips, but it will still likely be several years before we see Zeroth or TrueNorth products on the market. When they do finally come, these chips will enable companies to build new devices that can handle certain types of AI functions — such as image or speech recognition — at the chip level, without having to resort to higher level software or cloud services.

Kumar says of the training for a Zeroth chip application, that the initial training would happen in the cloud, but once the learning has been completed, the neural networks could be transferred to tiny, low-powered chips. These chips wouldn't be able to learn new tricks the way a true general AI could, but they would be able to take a considerable load off the main chips running in your device.

That could be a big deal for devices such as cell phones, wireless sensors, aerial drones, or a whole host of connected devices that need to use as little battery power as possible. But don't expect neuromorphic chips to replace all processors. Instead these chips — which Kumar calls "neural processing units" or NPUs — would complement today's CPUs (central processing units), much the same way GPUs (graphic processing units) do today.

Closer Than You Think

As science fiction author William Gibson once said: "the future is already here, it's just not evenly distributed." A world of AIs, drones, Virtual Personal Assistants and algorithms may seem far-fetched, but many technologies of the future world already exist in some form today, even if they're not yet commonplace.

We've already talked about Google's self-driving cars and their impeccable driving record. There are also drones that can already pilot themselves, computers that can analyze videos and images, machines that can process large volumes of data and information and produce written reports, or answer questions about it. It's not hard to conceive that in ten years' time these technologies will be ready for mass consumption, and will start to change our personal and professional worlds in amazing ways.

In his book *The Age of Spiritual Machines*, futurist Ray Kurzweil — now the head of one of

Google's AI projects — predicts that we'll have implants in our eyes and even brains. These neural implants, he anticipates, will enable direct brain-to-brain communication, and will enhance human intellectual capabilities.

Even more radically, he foresees that we'll have achieved human or near-human level AI by 2029. Machine intelligence will outclass humans in many ways, he writes, and there will be little — if anything — that humans can do better than machines.

In other words, by 2029, our AIs might not even need the input of human insights to achieve their goals. At that point the exponential rate of change starts to go vertical — with orders of magnitude of improvements in processing power every day, hour, minute and eventually second, as we head towards what has been termed a singularity.

It's hard to imagine the ways the world will change once we reach that level of AI. And while Kurzweil believes that AIs will help us create a better world, there are those who worry about what happens when machines become as smart as — if not smarter than — the rest of us.

AI as a New Utility

Kevin Kelly, founding editor of *Wired*, takes a more sober view of the next two decades.

He says that amid all this activity, a picture of our AI future is coming into view, and it is not the HAL 9000 — a discrete machine animated by a charismatic (yet potentially homicidal) human-like consciousness — or a Singularitarian rapture of super intelligence. His view is that the AI on the horizon looks more like Amazon Web Services —

cheap, reliable, industrial-grade digital smartness running behind everything, and almost invisible except when it blinks off. This common utility will serve you as much IQ as you want but no more than you need.

Kelly thinks that, like all utilities, AI will be supremely boring, even as it transforms the internet, the global economy and civilization. It will enliven inert objects, much as electricity did more than a century ago. Everything that we formerly electrified we will now cognitize. This new utilitarian AI will also augment us individually as people (deepening our memory, speeding our recognition) and collectively as a species. There is almost nothing we can think of that cannot be made new, different, or interesting by infusing it with some extra IQ, he believes.

What Risks Does AI Pose?

Stephen Hawking is one of the most brilliant scientists of our generation. And he's also one of the most pessimistic about the future of AI. Since at least 2001, Hawking has been warning the world that general AI could eventually pose an existential threat to humanity.

"The development of full artificial intelligence could spell the end of the human race. It would take off on its own, and re-design itself at an ever-increasing rate," Professor Hawking told the BBC in December 2014. "Humans, who are limited by slow biological evolution, couldn't compete, and would be superseded."

Yes, that sounds like the plot of movies like *Terminator* and *The Matrix*, but Hawking is far from alone in his concerns. At least two research

WHILE KURZWEIL BELIEVES THAT AIs WILL HELP US CREATE A BETTER WORLD, THERE ARE THOSE WHO WORRY ABOUT WHAT HAPPENS WHEN MACHINES BECOME AS SMART AS — IF NOT SMARTER THAN — THE REST OF US institutions have been founded to contend with the subject, including the Machine Intelligence Research Institute (funded in large part by PayPal founder and early Facebook investor Peter Thiel) and Oxford University's Future of Humanity Institute. More recently, Bill Gates, Steve Wozniak and Tesla Motors founder Elon Musk joined with many other experts at the Future of Life Institute's 2015 Conference in signing an open letter pledging to conduct AI research for the good of humanity — including ways of avoiding a *Terminator* style scenario.

But others, such as Dale Carrico, a lecturer in the Department of Rhetoric at the University of California, Berkeley, think Hawking and company are wrong to devote so much time and attention to such hypothetical problems — especially when compared with other more pressing concerns, such as global warming, pandemics, pollution and food security. "These lost seconds of attention and effort, these confused priorities and concerns, can and probably have already and most certainly will contribute very directly to lost lives," Carrico wrote on his blog in 2012.

But it's hard to completely dismiss the problem of hostile AI. In his book *Smarter Than Us: The Rise of Machine Intelligence*, Stuart Armstrong explains how quickly things could go wrong. For example, what if someone asked a general AI to "cure cancer" and the AI decided that the most expedient way to do that would be to kill all humans? How does one go about ensuring that these machines actually have our best interests in their silicon minds, given how hard it is for us to determine what's actually in our own best interests?

With the exception of autonomous weapons, it seems unlikely, at least at this juncture,

that even the strongest of AIs would actually have much agency in the world. How, exactly, would the hypothetical cancer-curing robot go about eradicating the human race, if its programming only allows it to provide answers or recommendations, and not actually act on the world? A machine with the ability to reprogram itself could, in theory, reprogram itself so that it can hack into computer systems and take over the world. But why exactly would it do so if its primary instructions are to provide information, rather than to take action? Still, as AI grows more complex, and inches closer to the world of general AI, many are thinking about what could go wrong — and how to stop it.

Another concern is that thanks to improvements in automation, AI could displace more jobs than it creates in coming years. After all, the creation of human-level AI is not required to build machines that can do certain tasks faster, or cheaper, than humans.

HISTORICALLY, NEW TECHNOLOGIES HAVE CREATED NEW JOBS, PREVENTING LONG-TERM MASS UNEMPLOYMENT. BUT THINGS MIGHT NOT WORK OUT THAT WAY AGAIN

"Everyone's talking about [the *Terminator* scenario] and no one is talking about the socioeconomic disruption," says Jeremy Howard, the founder of the artificial intelligence company Enlitic, which aims to create AIs that can help doctors diagnose diseases.

The most vulnerable jobs will be low-skilled positions — such as those in food service — but many others could be automated as well. Shockingly, a report by a group of Oxford University researchers published in 2013 concluded that 47 percent of all jobs were at risk of being replaced by AI within the next two decades. The implications for welfare and society cannot be overstated enough.

"If you think about what people do for work, most jobs require energy, perception, or judgement," Howard says. But thanks to the Industrial Revolution, tasks that require only energy have already been automated. Jobs that require only perception (such as data entry keyers and many manufacturing quality inspectors) will be the next to go, as computers get better at sensing the world through machine vision and other technologies. And with enough data, AIs could soon be able to help us make more and more decisions. "In some ways computers are already better at judgement," Howard says.

Even if a job can't be completely automated, if AIs can make people more effective — enabling one person to do the work of two or more people — then the job market will get squeezed. We're already starting to see this in the legal profession. In 2011, *The New York Times* reported that e-discovery software, which automates the process of scouring documents for information relevant to a particular case, is already able to do projects that could take dozens of lawyers and paralegals countless hours to complete. Not all legal work can be automated, but by eliminating a large number of jobs, e-discovery software makes the legal profession even more competitive.

Historically, new technologies have created new jobs, preventing long-term mass unemployment. But things might not work out that way again. And even if the world of AI creates many new jobs we have yet to imagine, the transition could be rough for those who do lose their careers.

This issue hasn't received as much attention as fears of a robot uprising, but researchers are starting to take a greater interest in the problem.

Determining the impact of AI on the labor market, and what policy responses may be necessary, are among the top priorities outlined by Musk and company in their open letter.

But perhaps we're all overestimating the rate of progress in AI. George Mason University economist Robin Hanson argues that based on current trends, we're more likely to see slow, steady progress in AI continue, rather than a super explosion of progress made in a short period of time. "AI researchers with 20 years of experience tend to see slow progress over that time, which suggests continued future slow progress," he wrote on his blog.

However, even small improvements to the technology that we have today could lead to big social changes. Even if Google doesn't succeed in creating a world full of autonomous cars, we could easily see a world of semi-autonomous vehicles that help us park, avoid accidents, and prevent us from breaking the law. That could lead to far fewer accidents — and less revenue from traffic tickets, insurance policies and repair shops.

Apply this line of thinking to every industry, and you'll realize just how big AI will be.

AI-Enabled Marketing: The Implications for Marketing

These advancements in AI are going to lead to major changes to the world. A large amount of change will be below the radar, such as businesses automating their processes. We won't see the AI impact, but we will feel it as we read and hear about how major businesses are shedding or re-styling their workforces.

The place where AI will become most visible will be in day-to-day consumer products — information-access, entertainment-centric and social-connection platforms accessed across multiple devices. And new categories of products that we cannot yet understand — potentially the more considered manifestations of IoT (Internet of Things) that offer a utility to justify the cost and the head-space required for consumers to consider them.

For premium products where the producer of content can demand it, these products will be accessed on a pay-model. But, based on what we have seen over the last decade, most of the information-access and social-connection products are most likely to be advertising and data-supported payment models.

That is why advertising, and therefore marketing, is most likely to be radically reorganized by this AI-revolution.

Although it is near-impossible to predict with accuracy how this landscape will look five to ten years from now, we can sense-out some likely scenarios using a logic-linked analysis. Put simply, if we start with what we know now, and simply ask the question "if that, then likely what?" If you ask this same question a few times you can start to see where things could go.

That is what we have done in this chapter — we have tried to peer beyond what we know. To scope out a commercially realistic view on the potential products we will be using and the advertising and data models that will likely support them. The point about it being commercially realistic is important; if money cannot be made, then neither will the technology.

We have started by taking a look at some of the likely products — and what they will do. We will also explore the new types of marketing and media opportunities that these products could offer up, and finally we take a broader view on what it may mean to plan marketing communications five to ten years from now.

The final point to make is that the focus here is on developed markets. Emerging markets will have aspects of what is covered, and the difference between the two will narrow as time goes by. Indeed it may very well be that emerging markets leapfrog entire stages of AI development by adopting technologies once they are established in developed markets — as has been the case with mobile phone penetration in emerging markets.

Here goes.

The Rise of the Sentient VPA

The operating system is where AI's impact will be most felt. Currently, when we consider consumer technology we have a device-centric mindset — we may think of our phones, laptops, tablets, or TV screens. That's because the operating systems are different. But if the operating system between them becomes identical, the focus will turn away from the type of screen and instead move to the operating system.

The changes we have seen with operating systems over the last few years have been in a very clear direction. That trajectory is best defined as a movement to reduce the gap between the external world and you. The gap can be seen in the effort required in having to search for information, having to remember a birthday, having to click into various sites to organize any activity. Much of the information is there but it requires us to cross a gap to get to it. We have to mentally flex ourselves out of shape in order to fit the disorganized, disconnected, decentralized world of information. Try missing a flight and having to change hotels, cancel your car, contact work colleagues, re-arrange diaries, call family members. We have to get our minds into the shapes of the different websites in order to operate them. Viewed from a position ten years from now, it will feel like a seamless bridge between us and the world was missing.

If you look at all the products being created today, they are skillfully trying to create that bridge — with map and navigation services, image-recognition features in social sites, recommendation engines and much much more.

THE PLACE WHERE AI WILL BECOME MOST VISIBLE WILL BE IN DAY-TO-DAY CONSUMER PRODUCTS — INFORMATION-ACCESS, ENTERTAINMENT-CENTRIC AND SOCIAL-CONNECTION PLATFORMS ACCESSED ACROSS MULTIPLE DEVICES

The most interesting bridging device, and the one that is likely to become the ultimate bridge, is arguably the Virtual Personal Assistant (VPA). At present they are very weak in their AI functionality — the voice recognition, although dramatically improved over the last few years, still requires us to flex ourselves out of shape. And their other functions are highly limited. But we must consider these through a lens of what they could become. Owners of ZX Spectrums or Commodore 64 computers, in the 1980s, would be amazed by the Xbox One and Sony PS4 games of today. What would that leap look like in these VPAs? What would a VPA have to be able to do to dumbfound today's users of Siri?

The answer lies somewhere in your VPA having, what is ostensibly, a sentient mind that spends its entire time and focus managing your life — making everything easier, removing boundaries.

Take for example, clicking on a link to be confronted with paragraphs of prose that often surround the key elements that you want to read. Or you may click on a link about how the oil price is going to affect housing shortage and when you get to the text it requires you to read paragraphs of padding before you get to the key points. Having an AI engine read, understand and then summarize it in a couple of highly crystalized points would offer enormous benefit.

The Ever-So Connected VPA

These VPAs will be much more than the walled gardens that they currently are. They will be open-ended VPAs — as in they will scan the tagged-up world. This is what Viv is working on creating ("Conversational Computing" p 37).

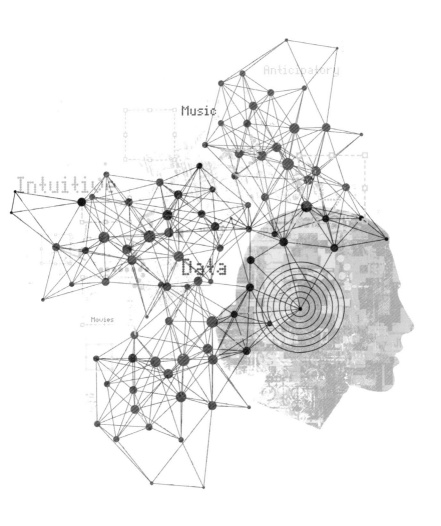

Opening up websites to search-engine crawlers is a good parallel to invoke here. The world will be opened up so that the VPAs can, through deep learning algorithms, understand everything — every ingredient, every possible way of booking/cancelling/amending/sending back, every location, what is in stock, the price, the performance, the review ratings, the sentiment and your contact's details and calendars.

The VPA will have access to the world and will edit it for you — our sense of what the internet is will dramatically contract from an unfathomably large expanse of information into a simple human voice. A voice that will most likely be accessed audibly, or via a more embedded form (the concept of implants are being explored by major technology companies). It may also manifest through other devices — handheld, wearable, in-car or devices in the world at large that recognize that it is you.

The question is: how will we use this Sentient-Virtual-PA?

Richer Connections

To try to project how we may interface with our Sentient-Virtual-PA (VPAs) we can look to a present-day analogy. Consider the representation of the personal assistant that is constantly on call and manages the complexities of life. They will alert you to let you know someone has called and summarize what they said and what they want — and ask you what you want to do. You would speak naturally back to them and they would understand and go back and communicate on your behalf. To extend the analogy further, they would be speaking to someone else's VPA and the two AIs would make all the necessary arrangements themselves.

This time-shifted and VPA-mediated form of communication is highly likely to be a new form of interaction and, over time, replace a large amount of live conversations. And with it are likely to come new forms of advertising. Again, imagine the real world PA signing off an exchange with a "oh, and the Chiswick Theater Company suggested you may want tickets to Hamlet next Tuesday — I have checked your diary and you are free. I was wondering if you want to invite Lexi, she is likely to say yes."

These prompts will likely be driven by a biddable advertising model where the message is created algorithmically in a completely native and natural way, as described above. The messages will be delivered when the quality-relevance score and the bid-price ratio trips a certain threshold. VPAs will only push through messaging that it deems relevant based on its knowledge about the individual it supports, meaning that only the most naturally relevant messaging will make it through.

Live communication could also be augmented with information and content that supports and adds to the conversation — here again, the biddable ad-model is very compelling.

Future models could take the form of suggested prompts that enhance the conversation, or make suggestions of things that you can do together.

It might suggest topics based on a combined interest graph or previous behavior. If you are talking about a UK-produced TV program called *Black Mirror* it would make the connection that the writer of the show was Charlie Brooker who also had a program called *2014 Wipe*, which you both had watched. It might then interject with:

OWNERS OF ZX SPECTRUMS OR COMMODORE 64 COMPUTERS, IN THE 1980S, WOULD BE AMAZED BY THE XBOX ONE AND SONY PS4 GAMES OF TODAY. WHAT WOULD THAT LEAP LOOK LIKE IN THESE VPAS? WHAT WOULD A VPA HAVE TO BE ABLE TO DO TO DUMBFOUND TODAY'S USERS OF SIRI?

"you both watched *2014 Wipe*, and if you're looking for something similar, you might both enjoy x."

This would be appropriate content to support with an ad-funded model similar to PPC (pay-per-click).

A company called Emu was pioneering this technology before it was purchased by Google at the end of 2014. Emu was, at heart, an IM (Instant Messaging) application, but it differentiated itself with smart features that incorporated a virtual assistant, not unlike Siri, to automate tasks based on your conversations — meaning you could do things like schedule appointments to your calendar, set reminders and even make reservations at a restaurant directly from your conversations.

THIS MOVEMENT TO A NATIVE ALGORITHM- DRIVEN MESSAGING PRODUCT WILL BE A HUGELY SIGNIFICANT CHANGE FOR MARKETING

Emu's roots were deep; its co-founder and CEO Gummi Hafsteinsson is ex-Google and ex-Apple, where he worked on Siri after coming on board following that startup's acquisition. Emu works a lot like Google Now, scouring your conversations for contextual information about your life and plans in order to provide recommendations about booking appointments, restaurant ratings and reviews, and even things like movie suggestions. In fact, Emu, which debuted as an Android application, looks like it could offer a lot to Google if the company is intent on continuing to grow the influence of Google Now across its properties.

From a media perspective, there is huge opportunity for entertainment and travel brands to book shared events — AI is therefore likely to become an important e-commerce gateway.

The messaging is likely to be algorithm-driven so it links directly to what is being discussed in a seamless way — the transaction will be where the money is made (so it may not even feel like an ad). For example, two people are talking about the cinema tonight and what time to meet and the VPA asks if you want a table for two at Nizuni on Charlotte Street in London at 6:30 p.m. A simple yes and it is automatically arranged via the VPA's links to booking engines, payment details and calendars.

This movement to a native algorithm-driven messaging product will be a hugely significant change for marketing. The bid price and relevancy/quality score are most likely to determine which brand, products or services are suggested. Feedback from the consumer about those brands' interactions — gleaned through VPA-overheard conversation — are likely to be a major factor in determining relevance/quality scores. They will do this in a more advanced way than the search algorithms of today, which are using social data to build quality scores. It is possible that the VPAs, as part of the value-exchange for being free, ask you what you thought of things you have just used or activities in which you have just taken part.

Knowledge-Based Targeting

Marketing opportunities won't just be based on live in-chat marketing. Post-chat marketing will be significant, using the semantic-data gleaned from the conversations.

This will provide rich data on the propensities of each audience for purchasing different categories, based not just on their intent but, for the first time, what they know and their opinions — a new dimension for segmenting and targeting.

The groundwork to enable this has arguably already started. For example, Yahoo has the power of

18 years of emails at its disposal, a remarkable 225 petabytes of unstructured data. The inbox is like a perfect digital memory that holds so much information about your personal life, whether it's photos, travel plans, online shopping orders or dinner reservations. With AI, the cross-platform targeting potential from this is simply remarkable.

For example, if we were planning the marketing communications for a new all-electric car we wouldn't just have a high propensity audience segment (a group of IP addresses collected from existing online click-behavior). We would also be able to address them at an individual level based on what they know, or don't know about electric cars and their very personal motivations for, or barriers to, purchase. But this is only part of it — with AI-engines, it is likely that brands will know what consumers are going to do before they do.

Preemptive Marketing: What Now for Free Will?

This level of data will allow for the advent of Preemptive Marketing. This is where individuals are algorithmically-identified as high-potentials based on patterns of behavior that are too complex for humans to identify. This type of analysis has already been successfully deployed in other areas such as predicting where crimes are more likely to happen. Preemptive Marketing will really only reach its full potential when we have the AI to extract the insights in the data.

The potential is that groups of individual IP-addresses or User-IDs will become high prospects for various products/services based on seemingly unrelated prior activities, such as conversations and online behaviors. This will finally allow data-

strategies to become much more sophisticated —
at present agencies select cookie-pools of people
captured from click-based activities over the last
few days or weeks, with no deep understanding if
that audience has already fulfilled on that purchase.

With Preemptive Marketing, it is not just the bid
that is real-time — the data will finally be real-
time too.

Winning the ability to be the suggested brand/
product for these prospects as they pop into a high-
propensity or an active-request state is going to be
of increasing and intense focus. The bid price and
quality score is going to be the crucial determinant
— along with speed.

The trading-floors of the major financial hubs are a
good early forerunner for where media is heading.
The movement to a live trading exchange in the
1980s is analogous to the movement media
agencies made to programmatic-buying. The new
trend in Wall Street is algo-trading. Those who use
algorithms to trade are now more effective than
traditional traders, and the algorithms that emerge
have even been given names like "The Boston
Shuffler." And with this technique — termed "high-
frequency trading" — comes speed. Trade speeds
are now measured in nanoseconds (one billionth
of a second), and banks rent offices nearest to
the exchanges so that they can shave off 100
nanoseconds in how long it takes from a commit to
buy/sell and the event taking place.

The identification and aggregation of multiple bids
for the right audience who are in an active-request
state means it is absolutely possible that speed
will become a final competitive advantage for media
agencies. Media pitch-consultants/auditors ten

THE
IDENTIFICATION
AND
AGGREGATION
OF MULTIPLE
BIDS FOR
THE RIGHT
AUDIENCE
WHO ARE IN
AN ACTIVE-
REQUEST STATE
MEANS IT IS
ABSOLUTELY
POSSIBLE
THAT SPEED
WILL BECOME
A FINAL
COMPETITIVE
ADVANTAGE
FOR MEDIA
AGENCIES

years from now may be assessing the speed, and of course, overall performance of the trading component in the agencies' recommended marketing-technology-stack.

And who sees what, when, in which order, across which device, with which message will be decided by algorithms. The advent of algo-driven planning and optimization is already happening and its genesis can currently be seen in what Forrester Research has recently termed Adaptive Marketing — where market-level modeling (including off-line and external factors) is being integrated with consumer level attribution (digital) into a single view that takes account of long-term and short-term effects. The next step will be integrating this into the programmatic-buying platforms. And then following that, creating a machine-learning algorithm to take over.

A SIGNIFICANT FOCUS FOR MARKETING WILL BE TO INFLUENCE THE ALGORITHM AND ENSURE THAT THE VPA IS SURFACING YOUR BRANDS/ PRODUCTS AHEAD OF YOUR COMPETITORS

The messaging for this activity will also most likely be algorithmically driven. The technology is already almost here. Right now, the most advanced DCO (Dynamic Creative Optimization) technologies already allow for different assets within an ad template — as in multiple headlines, images, offers, etc. — to be selected based on the ad's performance. This includes live data — prices that can change based on the audience's behavior. And DCO extends to video ads with different vignettes (sections of the content) being versioned based on the audience.

As well as a general increase in the adoption of such technologies, with the versioning being optimized based on knowledge-based cues, it is thought that the next evolution in this space is most likely to be the assets being created algorithmically.

Heralding Algorithmic-Created-Ads

When Google began translating websites into different languages, the Google scientists fed the machine with multiple translated documents and allowed the machine to "learn" how to map one language to another. The result was a machine that can translate websites into languages that Google's engineers cannot speak — the output was beyond any mind that had created it.

It is almost inevitable that algorithms, which chew through petabytes of speech text, will be able to write coherent text specific to the offer and the mindset of the audience.

In the next ten years it is unlikely that this will replace major brand campaigns and their positionings and propositions, but it is quite possible it will largely replace the offer/nudge-based creative messaging that makes up 40–50 percent of all advertising.

In this new world, headlines, combined with offers and images, will emerge in the relevant language and cultural context. We will see the creative work after it has already appeared and is still running across the globe. We will pin ads to the wall and say — "these have emerged as very powerful ads in the U.S., Europe, China and Mexico."

And of course, there will rarely be just one content unit that works — each one will be different.

Algorithmic-driven creative and knowledge-driven targeting will open up the potential to move beyond segmentation and focus on individual level messaging — so each person has a communication targeted specifically at them based on their unique situation (what they know, what they like, category purchase propensity, the brand purchase propensity, where they are in the purchase process).

Outsourced Decisioning

If you start with the likely scenario that our VPAs will be tasked with carrying out many of our day-to-day tasks, including searching for options, it's clear it is our VPAs that will be making decisions on which brands/products we should see.

A significant focus for marketing will be to influence the algorithm and ensure that the VPA is surfacing your brands/products ahead of your competitors.

Dag Kittlaus — one of the founders of Apple's Siri and now CEO of AI company Viv — gives the example of travel sites like Priceline. Today, these companies spend a lot of money advertising cheap rates on flights, hotels and rental cars. But if you have an AI assistant automatically checking every vendor for the best deals, the end consumer would never need to see such ads.

However, it is inevitable that it will go much further than this. As the VPA takes over more tasks, our choices and preferences will be learned by the software allowing preemptive decisions to be made on our behalf. The AI device will sift through all of the meta-data from brands and just decide for you. Again, imagine the personal assistant of today saying "I have sent your friend some flowers and arranged for you both to take the train to the airport...a car is going to pick you up at 5:45 a.m." For many purchase decisions, where there is little discernible difference between brands, the decision will simply be made by an algorithm.

It could alert you (and ultimately pre-order) daily items as it knows you're running short ("your toothpaste is nearly finished, I've added a new tube to your shopping basket"). It might also ask if you just want it to keep replacing items with the same brands as they run out so it doesn't have to ask you every time. The advanced AI device would also learn from your changing behaviors. If you started making more ethical choices about food purchases, it might make suggestions for different laundry detergents that fulfill your ethical criteria.

This may sound like a remarkable product innovation, but it won't work unless marketers are on board. This would involve opening access to AI assistants with all kinds of data about their products, tagged like content on a webpage optimized for search engines. Products in our typical grocery shop would need to have basic "tagged" information such as descriptors and price, but also where the product is from, what goes in to it, how the ingredients were sourced, and where it was shipped from, so our AIs can confidently recommend that product or service to us based on what it has learned about the kind of purchases we each prefer to make.

Indeed it is already the case that the choice of marketers to release data about their products isn't really a choice at all — the data already increasingly exists, so in reality it just needs to be aggregated.

Marketers will need to adapt. Instead of looking just to influence the consumer, they will also need to influence the algorithm. We will move to an era of marketing to the machine. There is a precedent for this in search engine optimization, which aims to maximize a website's visibility to Google and other search engines. VPA optimization is next.

MARKETERS WILL NEED TO ADAPT. INSTEAD OF LOOKING JUST TO INFLUENCE THE CONSUMER, THEY WILL ALSO NEED TO INFLUENCE THE ALGORITHM. WE WILL MOVE TO AN ERA OF MARKETING TO THE MACHINE

This will require "optimizing" review data, as this will be one of the primary contributors to the quality score algorithm that marketers can optimize. And not just optimizing it, but acquiring it in the first place.

Obtaining positive sentiment from customers will become the biggest determinant of whether the AI devices recommend it. Leading marketers will be category-best-in-class at optimizing to this KPI. Reviews and sentiment are going to be so important it may be that this becomes a new emerging marketing function.

Companies are now starting to emerge in this space — for example, Cluep is a Toronto startup with a patent-pending contextual-analysis engine that sorts social media users into emotional categories based on how they feel when they post. Advertisers can target mobile ads at people who've recently posted a happy, angry or sad tweet about their brand. This type of technology will allow marketers to target consumers that are the most likely to write positive reviews about a brand. This could be the start of targeting in the AI era.

The user experience will be important, as the sentiment — captured through overheard conversation and perhaps even a rating/review system — will assess the quality-relevance score for each product or brand.

By combining price comparison searching with social reviews, we could ultimately have a new 'quality score' algorithm. This could be further enhanced by actual usage data if the product is also a connected device. The quality score algorithm would ultimately draw in bid price from the advertiser, relevance of the product to the query, previous purchasing behavior of the end user, prices of the product, and a review score for the product along with usage data to validate the product's quality from the very people who have already purchased the item.

All of which will, of course, remain entirely invisible to users, who are merely presented with a couple of car hire options by their chirpy VPA.

IoT (Internet of Things)
As Product Assessors

This quality score could also be based on the actual performance of products — with data taken direct from source. For many products, the performance comparison cannot rely on what the end user thinks or feels. Consider laundry detergents that could be assessed on how clean clothes are by IoT washing machines, petrol quality assessed by cars, taxi services assessed by smart phones on how efficient they are at getting from a to b.

This performance data is going to become readily available via IoT, so there is a better than average chance that it will be utilized for assessing product performance.

Of course, a connected product will also be alerting the user's VPA when they are close to expiration or renewal — this will create a demand for the VPA to inform their user that the kettle is due a replacement and ask if they would like to see some options or if they want the VPA to just make the call. Depending on the category, thousands of these moments are happening every day and will be the focus on bid price, quality relevance scores and speed.

Privacy in an AI-World

Privacy anxiety is not a new issue; we have been voicing our concerns about this for at least a decade. We have all watched the outcomes of the various government-led directives. The striking observation is that, after an initial outrage, the majority of people just get used to sharing their data. In part this is because the value exchange is a good deal for the end user — they get access to world-class utility and content, and only have to view some personalized ads to get it.

But how will this change when the data being gleaned isn't just where you click, but based on what you actually say? This is the next epoch in data collection.

Google has filed a patent titled "Advertising based on environmental conditions" that enables an algorithm to listen in on phone calls. And in early 2015, the lead news story across the world was Samsung's new smart TV and a statement in its privacy policy which declares: "Samsung may collect, and your device may capture, voice commands and associated texts so that we can provide you with Voice Recognition features and evaluate and improve the features. Please be aware that if your spoken words include personal or other sensitive information, that information will be among the data captured and transmitted to a third party through your use of Voice Recognition."

It is the increasing concentration of such vast quantities of people's data into new media businesses and telecoms companies that has fueled U.S., U.K. and other government agencies' anxieties and policies — this is only going to become more complex.

With an AI-driven VPA, it is possible that a new model might arise that protects privacy without compromising the usefulness of data for advertisers. Today, ad targeting generally works something like this: a media-technology company, such as Google, collects massive amounts of data about you. That data is fed into servers, data is crunched, and a set of specifically targeted ads are sent back to your computer.

But in the future, that process may be inverted.

Privacy's Answer: Pull, Not Push

Instead advertisers, once all of their data is tagged, may simply set the bid price and the VPAs will actually make the decisions on when to pull down a brand/product and surface-up a suggestion to their user. Then it will report back to the advertising company which ads were actually shown so that the company can bill its clients.

Have you ever looked at a pair of shoes on an e-commerce site, only to find that ads for those sneakers following you around on other sites for months and months after you already bought them from another store? Well, your VPA will save you from ever seeing ads like that again, because it will know that you already bought new shoes, saving you the irritation of seeing pointless and repetitious ads, and the advertiser from wasting money on ads that will never move product.

In some ways, the VPA's ability to show you the exact right ad at the exact right time may seem creepy. But it will be far less creepy than thinking about a bunch of "unseen corporations" gathering massive amounts of data about you, and will help advertisers comply with EU law to boot.

WHEN ALL OF THIS COMES INTO EFFECT, WE WILL LIVE IN A WORLD WHERE VPAs ARE THE GATEWAYS BETWEEN US AND THE WORLD OF BRANDS

A startup called Kimera Systems is already hard at work on such a system. The idea is that all of your personal data would be under your control, and Kimera's software would only be able to use small amounts of data that you share with the company in order to help you find what you're looking for. Co-founder Mounir Shita argues that, given enough data about a single person, a virtual assistant could do as good a job, if not better, than a cloud-based system with large volumes of data about millions of different people. "The last thing the future of technology should do is to categorize you," he says. "I truly believe the power of intelligent peer-to-peer technology can deliver unique services to a single person while still turning a profit."

When all of this comes into effect, we will live in a world where VPAs are the gateways between us and the world of brands. For regular and lower-interest purchases, where there is little differentiation between products, the VPAs will make decisions and recommend (or autonomously purchase) on our behalf.

A New Role for Broadcast Communications

In this new world there is likely to be a new role for broadcast advertising, predicated on influencing sentiment/reviews and rating engines — leveraging behavioral principles to implicitly communicate that this brand is being highly rated. If audiences who are low-involvement are exposed to positive sentiment about a brand, they won't remember where they saw it, they will just have a sense of "that brand is good," which will influence how they discuss it and review it.

The KPI for this activity will be positive mentions of the brand across text or voice conversations;

this then impacts the quality score, which in turn increases likelihood of the brand being selected by the VPA and/or reduces the bid price required.

If this happens, expect to see a dramatic increase in quotes, reviews and qualified endorsement appearing in broadcast advertising.

Aside from this, there will, of course, still be an important role for classic-brand based communications — as a large percentage of products and services will be purchased as they are today. This marketing investment will be about affecting a non-rational response for decisions that are still made without the direct control of the VPA. These will be the higher-interest purchase decisions where the brand, and what it represents, is an important factor in a human decision.

This broadcast-outreach activity will be about generating fame and talk-ability in a much more ambitious way than today — it will appear to have disconnected itself from the world of marketing and moved in the direction of the world of entertainment.

Advertising Becomes Entertainment

In the future it may be harder to discern the difference between brands and entertainment platforms — TV programs, movies, entertainment spaces, branded-products, interactive-experiences.

The classic audio visual ad will become more of a brand spectacle.

The audio visual ad will go the same way as the retail sector. Trends in retail indicate that shopping will become 100 percent recreational. Retail will be exclusively a social and entertainment experience. In the same way that retail space will become "show rooms," TV/premium video ads will become more like the show room too.

Emotionally-powerful brand communication will be widely understood to be the most efficient way of driving long-term payback — its effect assessed within AI-driven attribution models. Because of this there will be an emotion war, with each brand experience attempting to elicit an emotional response — our endorphin, serotonin and oxytocin glands will become increasingly tolerant, and therefore the bar will keep getting higher.

Brace yourself. It will be like the U.S. Super Bowl mixed with the U.K. Christmas ad-break, on steroids. In more places, more of the time.

Strong-AI, 2029 and Algorithm-Driven Creativity

Machines are going to radically improve the way advertisers communicate their rational messaging to consumers, but what about the creative brand-led side of the business? Could a machine be as imaginative as a human, and create the next marketing campaign?

When we achieve strong-AI (AI that is as intelligent as a human) there is no reason to suggest that it couldn't create the next genre in art or music.

With deep learning, AIs could understand how political unrest stimulated the rise of punk music, and how artist Paul Cezanne's late work paved the way to the Braque/Picasso Cubist movement. In the same way that it might be able to predict

BRACE YOURSELF. IT WILL BE LIKE THE SUPER BOWL AD-BREAK ON STEROIDS. IN MORE PLACES. MORE OF THE TIME riots in a city if a certain number of variables are present at any point in time, it could recognize when the next paradigm shift is about to happen in a creative field, and specifically which traditions within the genre might be flexed, abolished or pushed further.

This, according to Kurzweil, is going to happen in 2029. At that point, it is quite possible that brilliant new creative work is conceived algorithmically. So, for now, let's assume that the first Cannes Lion to be won by an AI engine is at least 15 years away.

But that is simply replacing what we can already do with humans. It is perhaps more interesting to consider what could be done that we cannot currently do. One possible scenario is AIs fronting up creative campaigns themselves — to have a brand personality within, say, an online-display format that, if you choose, can speak to you. Imagine the potential for financial-service based business such as home-loan lenders to be able to start a dialogue with consumers and answer questions as naturally as a human would but with the ability to answer all of your questions and even complete a secure transaction. Your own VPA may even be there advising you of the veracity of what is being claimed.

We may witness brands designing their own sentient AI personalities. Try to imagine a sentient version of Aleksandr Orlov from CompareTheMarket.com (a U.K.-based advertising campaign) who had passed the challenging Turing Test with flying colors — it would truly be the ultimate in brand assets.

By that point, Strong AI will be strong indeed.

Marketing's AI Future

The more we depend upon AI software to handle tasks on our behalf, the more power we give to those AIs, and the smarter they will become. Ultimately, they will usher in the new world in which advertisers will need to operate. Technology will rule but creativity must not be sacrificed, despite the temptation to do so.

Optimizing to the machine will be the greatest determinant of success. Ensuring that the current disciplines of SEO, PPC and programmatic buying are being embraced and upskilled now will help in the future as these will be the most transferable skills to our new models.

Ultimately, there might be fewer messages seen, but the ones that do get seen will have been selected based on extremely specific purchasing and behavioral data about you. This will be combined with a bid price from the advertiser, a quality score for the product/service and usage data to confirm the product/service's experience. All of which will be handled in nanoseconds by our VPAs, and served up without us knowing which brands or products narrowly missed out.

And when done well, broadcast brand communication will take the form of spectacular content and experiences, indiscernible from entertainment.

5

Summary

AI could be the most significant invention in the history of humanity – and the ramp leading up to this starts now.

Today AI has already produced a universal translator, self-driving cars and computers that can write basic news stories, play video games and win at *Jeopardy*. Manufacturers are already developing computer chips that mimic aspects of the human brain.

As amazing as these are, they are still what we call "narrow AI." They're remarkably good at learning about one thing — such as driving or translating languages — but they can't learn to do anything else without significant reprogramming.

With the future development of Deep Learning, we are on the road to creating a general purpose AI that will be like consciousness in a box. We will be able to apply this intelligence to anything – as a utility.

And as Moore's Law marches on, doubling the raw power of computers while halving their price every 12–18 months, we'll start seeing super powerful

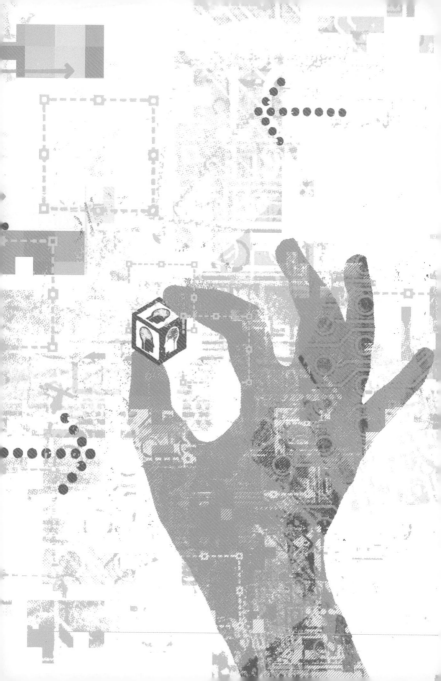

AI. By 2029 we may begin to see a new breed of even smarter AIs — what we call "strong AI." These machines will start to become smarter than humans. They will then take over the role of making themselves smarter. Once we reach that point — which some call "Singularity" — there's no telling what the future will hold.

Marketing will be at the forefront of this new world. Marketers are already using machine learning to target ads, to recommend products, and to sift through mountains of data collected in social media and even spot logos and other brand imagery in photos posted online.

However, as technology gets more sophisticated, we will see a transformation in the entire way we think about marketing and advertising – with human intervention removed from the micro-decisioning (channels, media units, copy, etc.) and elevated to the technology construction and data management level.

And the coming world of sentient Virtual Personal Assistants will create a completely different marketing environment. Many of us will simply let our VPAs do much of our shopping for us, forcing brands to compete in completely new ways. They will be the gatekeepers that we, as marketers, will need to influence. So instead of marketing directly to people, we will have to think about marketing to algorithms as well. Optimizing for word of mouth and creating killer products will be paramount.

The challenges are huge. But with those challenges come opportunities – where thinking and technology become the determinant of marketing success.

This book is about putting this new world, that we are all walking into together, on the agenda.

So that, as marketers, we can put in place the infrastructures now to be ready for this new reality and be more attuned to news of new developments as they emerge in the world around us — so we can be first to spot opportunities.

As individuals, we can start to consider how we, and our families, are going to flourish in this new sentient world.

Afterword

Scott Hagedorn
CEO Annalect

Imagine you had a friend that said the exact same thing to you, at the exact same decibel, ten to fifteen times in a row. Imagine a friend that never recognized you. Imagine a friend that never noticed what you were wearing. Never asked how your kids were. Never asked what you are interested in. Instead, this friend would just drone on in monotony about themselves while you continually drop hints around what you'd like to talk about. This friend is shallow, self-absorbed and not self-aware. You would probably like to slap this "friend" around the face.

This is how brands behave.

The concept of one-size fits all branding is horribly outdated.

The concept of a company's communication efforts becoming sentient is something for the future. But there is much we can do, right now.

The majority of website browser users do not turn off cookies even though the opportunity to opt-out is present. Why? One theory is that they, like I, are not as concerned about personalized ads as many think. When presented with tailored ads they actually find it to be useful. Users, especially of the younger cohorts, understand the quid pro quo of the internet and therefore they are willing to trade their data for the amazing utility that has been created.

If I've just purchased something from your site or store, I want your company to acknowledge that. Please figure out what product would surprise and delight me and put that in front of me next. If I already subscribe to your services, there is no need to talk to me unless you want to sell me something else or you think I'm likely to churn. If you suspect that I'm more likely to buy something after work, versus in the middle of the day, serve me up something then. Inform me when I am most likely to want information and, perhaps, entertain me when I am in a relaxed state – utilizing the different platforms and technologies to enhance the trans-device dialog.

These are some simple business rules that can exist in the latest ad tech platforms that, as well as dramatically improving the consumer experience, can also save you money. The worlds of customer relationship management (CRM) and addressable media have collided and we are all just waking up to that now. All channels are CRM informed. The magic in marketing currently is about using data and technology to make decisions. When you spot a prospect do they look like they could be high value and should you bid more? Did they just buy a car and is it time to serve them an auto insurance ad? What message should you

send? Decisions that can now be made at an individual level, with individual tailored messaging – within a fraction of a second.

As excited as I am for the future of sentient communications programs, I call to all of you marketers out there, client or agency folk, to invest in these simple interim steps. Write out the simple business rules on how you want your communications to behave. Build up a suite of content capable of having a multi-variant dialog with an audience. Mine your customer data to get a better feel of what they are interested in and what they are most likely to be interested in next. And use this to create a cutting-edge marketing infrastructure that can radically reorganize your competitors. And make consumers' lives a little more enjoyable.

C'mon brands! Don't make me slap you around the chops.

Annalect is an Omnicom Media Group company that provides clients with data-driven marketing strategies powered by a connected system of technology

CHAPTER 1
INTRODUCTION: What Exactly is Artificial Intelligence?

Bishop, Chris, interview

Finley, Klint, 'Microsoft's Futuristic New Tool Translates Skype Calls in Real Time', Wired, May 28th 2014

Gomes, Lee, 'The Self-Driving Google Car May Never Actually Happen', Slate, October 21st 2014

Gowan, Michael, 'LG Smart Fridge Spots Spoiled Food, Orders Groceries', TechNewsDaily, January 4th 2013

Hayes, Tyler, 'The Grid Is The Website Of The Future: It Builds Itself', Fast Company, October 20th 2014

Kelly, Kevin, What Technology Wants, Penguin Books, September 27th 2011

Kelly, Kevin, 'The Three Breakthroughs That Have Finally Unleashed AI On The World', Wired, October 27th 2014

Kelly, Kevin, 'The Future Of AI? Helping Human Beings Think Smarter', Wired, December 3rd 2014

Orlowski, Andrew, 'CAPTAIN CYBORG: The Wild-Eyed Prof Behind 'Machines Have Become Human' Claims', The Register, June 10th 2014

Steiner, Susie, 'Smart Fridge? Idiot Fridge, More Like', The Guardian, January 11th 2012

The Associated Press, 'Uber, Carnegie Mellon Partnering On Pittsburgh Research Lab', NYTimes.com, February 3rd 2015

CHAPTER 2
THE ROAD TO INTELLIGENCE:
Where It Started and the Road Leading to Today

Bosker, Bianca, 'SIRI RISING: The Inside Story Of Siri's Origins – And Why She Could Overshadow The Iphone', The Huffington Post, January 24th 2013

Coker, Mark, 'Startup Advice For Entrepreneurs From Y

Combinator' VentureBeat, March 26th 2007

Delo, Cotton, 'Startup Watch: Gazemetrix Lets Brands See If
Logos Are Present In Instagram Photos', Ad Age,
December 11th 2012

Finley, Klint. 'Facebook Says It Knows Where People Are
Migrating — But Can You Trust Its Data?'. Wired,
December 26th 2013

Finley, Klint, 'Out In The Open: Free Software That Teaches
Your Smartphone How To See', Wired, June 24th 2014

Hammond, Kris, interview

Hawkins, Jeff, interview

'IBM100 - Deep Blue', IBM.com, n.a

Kittlaus, Dag, interview

Kumar, Samir, phone interview

Kurzweil, Ray, The Age of Intelligent Machines, MIT Press,
March 19th 1992

Kurzweil, Ray, The Age of Spiritual Machines, Penguin Books,
January 27th 2000

Kurweil, Ray, The Singularity is Near, Gerald Duckworth & Co
Ltd, March 9th 2006

Levy, Steven, 'Can An Algorithm Write A Better News Story
Than A Human Reporter?', Wired, April 4th 2012

Levy, Steven, 'Siri's Inventors Are Building A Radical New AI
That Does Anything You Ask', Wired, December 8th 2014

Linden, David J., 'The Singularity Is Far: A Neuroscientist's
View', Boingboing, July 14th 2011

Lyons, Daniel, 'Ray Kurzweil Wants To Be A Robot', Newsweek,
May 16th 2009

Marcus, Gary, 'Is "Deep Learning" A Revolution In Artificial
Intelligence?' The New Yorker, November 25th 2012

Markoff, John, 'Scientists See Advances In Deep Learning, A Part Of Artificial Intelligence', New York Times, November 23rd 2012

McMillan, Robert, 'The Incredible AI That Can Watch Videos And Tell You What It's Seeing', Wired, May 2nd 2015

'Memorial Sloan Kettering Trains IBM Watson To Help Doctors Make Better Cancer Treatment Choices', published by Memorial Sloan Kettering Cancer Center', April 11th 2014

Modha, Dharmendra S., 'Introducing a Brain-inspired Computer', IBM Research

Novet, Jordan, 'Google Acquires Jetpac, A Photo Startup With Artificial-Intelligence Smarts', VentureBeat, August 15th 2014

Oremus, Will, 'The First News Report On The L.A. Earthquake Was Written By A Robot', Slate, March 17th 2014

Pharyngula, 'Ray Kurzweil Does Not Understand The Brain', scienceblogs.com, August 17th 2010

Ptolemy, Barry, Transcendent Man: The Life and Ideas of Ray Kurzweil (documentary film), Ptolemaic Productions in partnership with Therapy Content, 2011 (U.S. release)

Rennie, John, 'Ray Kurzweil's Slippery Futurism', IEEE Spectrum, November 29th 2010

Russell, Stuart J., and Norvig, Peter, Artificial Intelligence: A Modern Approach, 3rd ed. Pearsons, December 11th 2009

Shiftan, Nick, and Gupta, Abu, phone interview

Simonite, Tom, 'A Brain-Inspired Chip Takes to the Sky', MIT Technology Review, November 4th 2014

Spencer, Leon, 'ANZ To Tap Watson For Big Data Financial Advice', ZDNet.com, October 8th 2014

'The Deep Mind Of Demis Hassabis', Medium, April 29 2015

Armstrong, Stuart, 'Smarter than us: The rise of Machine Intelligence', Machine Intelligence Research Institute, May 1st 2014

Carrico, Dale, 'Insecurity Theater: How Futurological Existential-Risk Discourse Deranges Serious Technodevelopmental Deliberation', Amor Mundi, 2012

Cellan-Jones, Rory, 'Stephen Hawking Warns Artificial Intelligence Could End Mankind', BBC, December 2nd 2014

Frey, Carl, 'The Future of Employment: How Susceptible are Jobs to Computerisation?', Oxford Martin Programme on the Impact of Future Technologies, September 17th 2013

Hanson, Robin, 'I Was Wrong', Overcomingbias, January 21st 2014

Howard, Jeremy, interview

Markoff, John, 'Armies Of Expensive Lawyers, Replaced By Cheaper Software', NYTimes.com, March 4th 2011

Associated Press, 'Physicist Warns Humans About A.I.', newsletter, n.a

Abraham, Jay, 'Use Preemptive Marketing To Make Customers Think Of You First', Early To Rise, May 29th 2015

Etherington, Darrell, 'Google Acquires Emu, An IM Client With Siri-Like Intelligence', Tech Crunch, August 6th 2014

Finley, Klint, 'The Internet Of Anything: A Virtual Assistant For Your Gadgets, From Phones To Refrigerators', Wired, January 26th 2015

Hof, Robert D.,'Deep Learning', MIT Technology Review', April 23rd 2013

Winarsky, Norman, and Mark, Bill, 'The Future Of The Virtual Personal Assistant', Tech Crunch, March 25th 2012